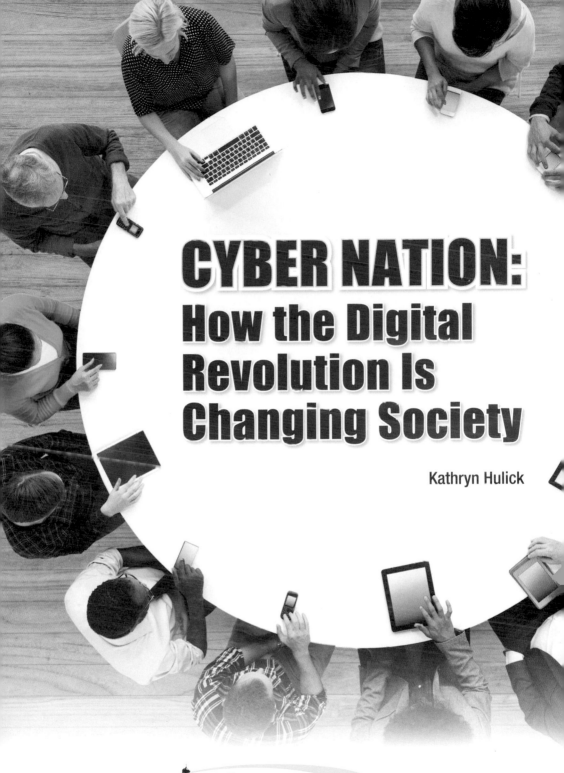

CYBER NATION:
How the Digital Revolution Is Changing Society

Kathryn Hulick

ReferencePoint
Press®

San Diego, CA

About the Author

Kathryn Hulick began her career with an adventure. She served two years in the Peace Corps in Kyrgyzstan, teaching English. She did not have a cell phone and had to travel for half an hour by taxi to use the Internet. But since her return to the United States, she embraced digital technology and began writing books and articles for kids. Technology and robots are some of her favorite topics. Look for her books *Careers in Robotics*, *How Robotics Is Changing the World*, and *Robotics and Medicine*. She also contributes regularly to *Muse* magazine and the Science News for Students website. She enjoys hiking, painting, reading, and working in her garden. She lives in Massachusetts with her husband, son, and dog.

For more information, contact:
ReferencePoint Press, Inc.
PO Box 27779
San Diego, CA 92198
www.ReferencePointPress.com

LIBRARY OF CONGRESS CATALOGING-IN-PUBLICATION DATA

Name: Hulick, Kathryn, author.
Title: Cyber Nation: How the Digital Revolution Is Changing Society/by Kathryn Hulick.
Description: San Diego, CA: ReferencePoint Press, [2019] | Audience: Grade 9 to 12. | Includes bibliographical references and index.
Identifiers: LCCN 2018013569| ISBN 9781682824696 (hardback) | ISBN 9781682824702 (eBook)
Subjects: LCSH: Internet—Social aspects—Juvenile literature. | Online social networks—Juvenile literature. | Group identity—Juvenile literature.
Classification: LCC HM851 .H85 2019 | DDC 302.30285—dc23
LC record available at https://lccn.loc.gov/2018013569

CONTENTS

A Whole New World

Ryley Aceret sealed his cell phone inside an envelope. He and hundreds of his classmates at a private school in San Francisco had agreed to give up all electronic devices for three days as part of a Tech Timeout Challenge. The goal was to explore what it feels like to be without these devices. Each student who chose to participate put his or her phone in a large envelope and agreed not to use any electronic device for the entire three days. Many did not make it. Aceret, a high school senior, gave up the very first night and ripped open his envelope. "I felt normal again," he says. "When I wasn't with my phone I felt different, like I was naked all the time."[1]

This story illustrates the extent to which digital technology has pervaded people's lives. They tend to feel anxious, bored, and lonely when their devices are not available. They often carry a phone around in a pocket all day long and sleep with it at night, as if it is an extension of the body. "I sleep with my phone on my pillow. It's the first thing I reach for when I wake up in the morning,"[2] says Henry Button, a sixteen-year-old from Essex in the United Kingdom.

Many young people have no idea what it is like to live without smartphones and similar devices. Even adults who remember life without digital technology have become deeply accustomed to having constant access to the Internet, social media, text messaging, games, and more. Some people are so enamored with Instagram that they have named their babies after photo filters, including Lux, Amaro, Reyes, and Juno. People today are used to having all their friends and family a quick text away. When they need to get somewhere or schedule something, they tap an app.

Many young people today do not know what it is like to live without smartphones. They often carry them around in their pockets all day and sleep with them at night, as if they are an extension of the body.

When they need the answer to a question, they Google it or ask a virtual assistant such as Siri or Alexa.

The Digital Revolution

One important feature distinguishes a digital device from most of the other appliances and tools in our lives: Internet access. The ability to go online from a phone, tablet, car, toy, or appliance turns the object into a means of connection and communication. Smartphones and other mobile technology have helped spread the Internet around the world at a brisk pace. As of 2017 half of the world's population had Internet access, a 10 percent increase since 2016, according to the *Digital in*

"When I wasn't with my phone I felt different, like I was naked all the time."[1]

—Ryley Aceret, high school senior

2017: Global Overview report from the social media consulting companies We Are Social and Hootsuite. The same report found that 66 percent of the people in the world now use a mobile phone, an increase of 30 percent over the previous year.

In addition, people who use the Internet are spending more and more time online. In 2000 the average American spent around 9.4 hours online every week. By 2017 that number had jumped to 24 hours per week, according to a report from the Annenberg School for Communication and Journalism at the University of Southern California. The fact that many people now carry Internet-connected devices everywhere they go helps explain this increase. The most common online activities are browsing the web, using social media, listening to music, playing games, and watching videos.

The Internet is available anywhere, at any time. This convenience has prompted activities such as personal communications, shopping, banking, business meetings, event planning, and more to move online. Many people and businesses also store important documents and files online in the cloud, a name for any digital storage system that allows continual access from any device.

A Human Right

Internet access has become so important that many experts argue it is no longer appropriate to consider it a luxury. People need digital technology and Internet access to participate fully in modern life. "You can't be a functioning adult and remain unconnected,"[3] says Dan McGarry, media director at the *Vanuatu Daily Post*. A 2015 report from the Broadband Opportunity Council, formed by former US president Barack Obama, said that broadband Internet access should be considered a core utility, alongside water, sewer, and electricity.

Consider the trouble people have leading their lives when the electricity goes out after a disaster. Losing access to the Internet can be just as problematic, severely limiting a person's ability to go about his or her daily tasks. The Internet is so important in to-day's world that the United Nations Human Rights Council voted in 2016 to make Internet access a human right. Any country that intentionally disrupts its citizens' access to the Internet is now considered to be in violation of their rights.

Internet access is a human right that is changing what it means to be human. Constant access to a digital world is altering human relationships, the economy, the flow of information, and even the concept of personal identity. Many of these changes are positive. For example, digital technology brings people closer together, essentially erasing physical distances. But other changes are troubling. Digital technology also pushes people apart, providing a virtual hiding place that may be more enticing than the real world. Both those who worry about the advance of digital technology and those who embrace it will have to find ways to adjust as the digital revolution becomes an ever more important part of reality.

CHAPTER ONE

Real Relationships

A family sits at the dinner table. During the meal, the father scrolls through Twitter. The mother taps a quick answer to a work e-mail. The son comments on a celebrity's Instagram post, and the daughter invites a friend to play a puzzle game. Each person is physically present in the same space. They are sharing the same meal. Yet they are also each absent, off in their own virtual worlds. No matter how good a person thinks he or she is at multitasking, being present in a virtual space almost always means temporarily ignoring the real world. This is merely one of many ways in which digital technology is changing the way people build and maintain relationships with each other.

Humans are social animals. They naturally yearn for connection with each other. Strong relationships enhance a person's happiness and general well-being. Digital technology offers myriad ways to connect, including texting; photo and video sharing; video calls; social media sites such as Facebook, Twitter, and Instagram; online forums and comment streams; and multiplayer gaming. Each of these channels comes with its own nuances. Each can foster healthy, happy relationships or host harmful, bullying behavior. It all depends on how people use the technology.

The Rise of Social Media

Before the 1970s, relationships formed through in-person experiences, postal mail, or phone calls. Over the next few decades, the beginnings of the Internet were established. This new communication medium opened many novel ways for people to talk to each other. Early e-mail and text messaging usually connected just a few people at a time in private exchanges. Social media was different, making it possible to easily stay in touch with a wide group of people, and in a more public manner. As of 2014 the average American adult Facebook user had 338 friends, according to the Pew Research Center. Social media sites help satisfy people's hunger for attention and connect them to others with similar interests. Today YouTube and Facebook are the second- and third-most visited websites in the world, trailing only Google in popularity.

The more people who create profiles and share content, the more successful a social media site will be. Numerous sites have tried to gain a following, only to fail. Friendster, Google+, and iTunes Ping never caught on. A social media site without enough users is like a party without enough guests: It will not be fun, and the guests will soon look for somewhere else to hang out.

Missing the Party

For many groups of friends, social media really is a virtual party. When not together in real life, they hang out online. The exchanges that happen in Instagram comments or while gaming together

Digital technology is changing the way people communicate and relate to each other. Today many families are distracted during family meals by texts, video clips, or work e-mails.

become part of real-life interactions, so much so that missing out on a friend's update may lead to exclusion or embarrassment. Today making or keeping friends in real life may be nearly impossible without also connecting online. The ability to go online is essential to many young people's social lives.

In 2016 the British newspaper the *Guardian* asked a group of teenagers to go without digital technology for as long as they could. Henry Button made it for seven days. When some online drama happened in his group of friends, he had no idea what was

Saving Lives

In March 2015 Andrew Parker posted a suicide note on his blog. "Nothing brings me joy," he wrote. "Everything I look at or think about only brings more pain. . . . I just can't keep going on like this. I can't. I can't. I can't." Parker was a thirty-four-year-old freelance writer who had struggled with anxiety and depression since he was a child. He put a link to the post on Twitter, and immediately, responses came pouring in. Friends, acquaintances, and even total strangers reached out. He wound up going to a treatment center and getting help. "Social media, those people, saved my life," Parker said. "I would not have sought help if I had not seen those messages. That was more than I could have asked for."

Organizations that work to prevent suicide realize that social media messages often precede an attempt. The fact that many people always have a digital device nearby means that someone should be able to respond instantly to a person in distress. The National Suicide Prevention Lifeline has worked with both Facebook and Twitter to make it easy for users to report a suicidal post. This then alerts a trained counselor to attempt to get in touch with the person. In addition, Lifeline worked with Google to make its phone number appear when individuals type in phrases that indicate they may be considering suicide. In this way, digital media has the power to bring a person who feels isolated and worthless back from the brink of disaster.

Andrew Parker, "The End of All Things," *Even If It Kills Me* (blog), March 17, 2015. https://andrewjparkerblog .wordpress.com.

Quoted in Laura Armstrong, "'Social Media Saved My Life,' Says Man of the Caring Responses to His Suicide Note," *Toronto Star*, April 9, 2015. www.thestar.com.

going on. The sixteen-year-old says, "I wouldn't turn [my phone] off again. Even though I was more productive, I felt a lot more isolated."[4] Janice Da Costa, an eighteen-year-old, literally missed a party during the challenge. She never found out about a friend's birthday celebration.

The irony here is that people who spend all of their time on digital media may feel more socially connected and fulfilled, but they often end up missing out on real experiences. "If you're spending three, four, or five hours a day in an online game or virtual world . . . there's got to be someplace you're not," says Sherry Turkle, a social scientist at the Massachusetts Institute of Technology (MIT). "And that someplace you're not is often with your family and friends."[5] If Da Costa had attended that birthday party, chances are good that many of her friends would have spent a good chunk of their time together texting, sending snaps, or checking Instagram rather than talking.

Texting Versus Talking

Some people go so far as to avoid in-person conversations in favor of digital communication. Sending and receiving text messages is now the most common means of communication for Americans younger than fifty, according to a 2014 Gallup poll. The younger a person is, the more likely he or she is to prefer texting, e-mail, and social media over phone calls. "There has been a shift in the way we communicate; rather than face-to-face interaction, we're tending to prefer mediated communication," says Paul Booth, assistant professor of media and cinema studies at DePaul University in Chicago. "We'd rather e-mail than meet; we'd rather text than talk on the phone."[6]

> "There has been a shift in the way we communicate. . . . We'd rather e-mail than meet; we'd rather text than talk on the phone."[6]
>
> —Paul Booth, assistant professor of media and cinema studies, DePaul University

Some people do not have the patience for real-time conversations. They want to know what is going on with other people—

but on their own terms. Texting and social media allow users a lot of control over their interactions with others, Turkle points out. A person can make a connection with someone without having to get too close or listen for too long. Turkle says, "Digital connections . . . may offer the illusion of companionship without the demands of friendship."[7] Friendship means opening oneself up to another person. Each person must focus on the other and listen, rather than just think about what he or she wants to say.

Obsession and Addiction

Most people understand the value of real-life conversations and experiences with other people. So they try to maintain a reasonable balance between time spent online and time spent in real life with loved ones. But it can be all too easy to pick up a smartphone at the dinner table. Many relationships between parents and children, husbands and wives, and boyfriends and girlfriends have suffered because one or both people spend too much time online. When a person pulls out his or her phone, it often makes loved ones feel slighted, ignored, or neglected.

Some people have developed extremely unhealthy obsessions with social media, video games, or other digital technology. Brooke, a teenager from California, was twelve when she got her first smartphone. She quickly became obsessed. She had multiple accounts on many social media sites. "It was always about refreshing my feed and I'd stay up until like 4:30 in the morning,"[8] she says. Her parents tried taking her phone away, but she would just find a way to get another one. Brooke eventually wound up receiving help at a treatment center for mental health issues that included excessive use of social media.

Such an extreme level of obsession with social media is unusual, but many people feel that they use digital technology more than they should. A 2012 survey by Common Sense Media found that 41 percent of people who own mobile phones described themselves as "addicted" to the technology. Medically, addiction is a disease with physical withdrawal symptoms. A better way to talk about the problem is as compulsive use or overuse of technology.

The main thing that feeds compulsive social media use is the positive attention users get from others. Several scientific studies have shown that social media interactions seem to be associated with the release of two brain chemicals, oxytocin and dopamine. Oxytocin, also called the "cuddle chemical," is released when people hug or kiss their loved ones. It is associated with happiness and trust. Dopamine is released in anticipation of a pleasurable experience and makes the person want to pursue the reward. Mauricio Delgado, a psychologist at Rutgers University in New Jersey, explains that as a person gets used to the positive feelings associated with "likes" and comments on social media, his or her brain begins to anticipate those feelings. "Often, if you have the earliest predictor of a reward—a sign of a social media alert, like your phone buzzing—you get a rush of dopamine from that condition stimulus,"[9] he says. As a result, it is nearly impossible to resist picking up the phone to see what the alert was for. The person's brain automatically seeks out the social reward of a new "like" or comment.

Ideal Lives

Positive online interactions make people feel good. Social media also gives users control over the content they share. People usually try to maximize positive feedback by curating a particular self-image. Often, people only share the most perfect moments of their lives. For example, a trip to the beach may include getting stuck in traffic, losing an expensive pair of sunglasses, and a horrible fight between two friends. But the photo everyone sees is a picture of the two friends smiling happily against a perfect ocean

Positive online interactions make people feel good. Often social media users try to maximize positive feedback by posting only the most perfect moments in their lives and leaving out any negative or embarrassing details.

sunset, a few hours before the fight. Turkle says, "We can edit our messages until they project the self we want to be."[10] People post the best moments from their lives in order to get positive attention from others.

Unfortunately, seeing so much perfection online makes many people feel inadequate and anxious. Evelyn Green, an eighteen-year-old from Durham, United Kingdom, says, "People only put good bits of life online and, even though you know this, you still see their 'perfect' lives and it makes you think yours isn't."[11] There is a lot of pressure to live up to what friends, family, and even strangers post. Seeing pictures of fantastic vacations, fad diets, and fancy clothing styles makes a teen feel that he or she needs to have those things, too, in order to fit in. "It feels like you're sold a life and are expected to live up to a standard that is impossible to achieve,"[12] says Nafeesa Deen, a nineteen-year-old from Buckinghamshire, United Kingdom.

Most teens and young adults measure their success on social media by the number of followers they have and the number of "likes" they get on their photos and other updates. To maintain an image of popularity, they may delete posts that did not get enough likes. "A lot of people can't cope with the anxiety if they see someone has criticized a photo, or posted a picture that looks better than theirs,"[13] says Julia Peters, a twenty-two-year-old from Leicestershire, United Kingdom. Positive feedback on social media makes people feel really good, but that is unfortunately not the only possible outcome. When a post receives very little feedback, a person may feel insecure, inadequate, and jealous of others. And negative feedback online may lead to feelings of rejection, sadness, or even depression.

> "People only put good bits of life online and, even though you know this, you still see their 'perfect' lives and it makes you think yours isn't."[11]
>
> —Evelyn Green, age eighteen, Durham, United Kingdom

Hiding Behind Emoticons

Online interactions lack many of the features of real-life conversations. Social cues such as facial expressions, gestures, and tone of voice are largely absent. People use emoticons as a way to fill in some of the missing information, but these smiling, blushing, or surprised faces are poor replacements for actually hearing and seeing another person laugh, gasp, or cry. As a result, in digital interactions, people's emotions tend to be invisible, meaning that they feel less empathy for each other. It is easier to say mean or hurtful things.

A digital argument shields the participants from the brunt of each other's sadness and anger. And each person can take time deciding how to respond or ignore a message if things get too uncomfortable. Though this may feel like a reasonable approach to navigating an argument, experts caution against it. "Whenever I hear stories of romantic break-ups, firings, or even arguments going on electronically, I cringe," says Alex Lickerman, a primary care physician in Chicago. "In-person interactions, though more difficult, are more likely to result in positive outcomes and provide opportunities for personal growth."[14]

Research has shown that selfish traits are increasing among young people, while skills associated with empathy and emotional intelligence are decreasing. Sara Konrath, a psychologist at the University of Michigan, found that college students in 2010 were less likely than students in previous years to agree with statements such as "I sometimes try to understand my friends better by imagining how things look from their perspective."[15] The students scored 40 percent lower on a standard test of empathy skills than students from the 1970s. The rise of digital technology may be causing a drop in emotional intelligence.

Cyberbullying

A lack of empathy can lead to misunderstandings or unintended harm. A person may post a comment or send a text, then go about his or her day under the illusion that the message was no big deal. Meanwhile, someone somewhere may be seething with anger, sobbing into a pillow, or blushing with shame after reading the message. "People clearly have a penchant for saying things in the electronic world they'd never say to people in person because the person to whom they're saying it isn't physically present to display their emotional reaction,"[16] says Lickerman.

In an episode of online harassment, strangers send unkind messages, insults, or threats to someone who has done or said something polarizing. Usually, the target did not intend his or her message to reach such a wide audience. Trolling, on the other hand, is when someone says mean or provocative things on purpose in order to provoke an angry response. Cyberbullying is similar to harassment, but the bullies and the victim often know each

Deadly Bullying

Kenneth Weishuhn Jr. was fourteen years old when he came out as gay. Soon afterward his classmates began teasing and bullying him. They created a hate group against gays on Facebook and sent Kenneth threatening text messages. "People that were originally his friends, they kind of turned on him," said his sister Kayla Weishuhn. "A lot of people, they either joined in or they were too scared to say anything." Within a few months the awful treatment had become too much. The young teen took his own life.

Unfortunately, Weishuhn is not the only young person to commit suicide after relentless online bullying. Almost half of suicides among young people are related to bullying, according to a 2010 study by the British charity BeatBullying. Mallory Grossman was only twelve when she killed herself in 2017. She had been told she was a loser and had no friends. Her mother, Diane Grossman, had tried to stop the harassment by talking to the school and to other parents. But one bully's mother reportedly said it was all just a big joke. And the school had not filed any reports about the incidents.

Most teens who become victims of cyberbullying survive. But the emotional scars may last the rest of their lives. The website StopBullying.gov offers resources to help people who are going through a cyberbullying ordeal. The National Suicide Prevention Lifeline is at 1-800-273-8255.

Quoted in KTIV, "Family: Bullies Pushed NW Iowa Teen to Take Own Life," April 16, 2012. www.ktiv.com.

other in real life. The authors of *Bullying Beyond the Schoolyard* define the act as "willful and repeated harm inflicted through the use of computers, cell phones, and other electronic devices."[17] Cyberbullies target a specific victim with repeated hurtful comments. In a 2015 study in *JAMA Pediatrics*, 23 percent of teens reported being victimized, while 15 percent admitted that they had bullied someone else online.

Children and teens have always picked on and bullied each other. However, digital technology changes the dynamic. "Cyberbullying is marked by its persistence," says Nicholas David Bowman, assistant professor of communication studies at

An online comment can lead to unintended harm. Often social media users do not consider that their posts will cause someone pain and embarrassment or reach a wide audience.

West Virginia University. "The bullying messages don't stay in a particular space, such as a playground, but can follow the child home."[18] A bully today has many more opportunities for contact with the victim. It is nearly impossible for the victim to escape unwanted attention. Cyberbullying is strongly linked to depression, and in the most extreme cases, victims have committed suicide.

Empowerment and Support

Cyberbullying is a real and disturbing problem. But social networks of supportive friends have also saved teens who had been considering suicide. People have the power to make each other terribly unhappy, but they can also support each other and boost each other's moods. Emotional support is much more effective in person or even over the phone than through text-based media. However, digital media can still help people feel better. A 2016 study by researchers at Facebook and Carnegie Mellon University found that people who received sixty or more personalized Facebook comments from close friends and family in a month also showed improvement in measures of happiness and life satisfaction. "It turns out that when you talk with a little more depth on Facebook to people you already like, you feel better,"[19] says study author Robert Kraut, a professor of human-computer interaction at Carnegie Mellon University.

And those positive feelings may spread through a person's network. A 2014 study by researchers at the University of California–San Diego found that negative and positive expressions of emotions both tend to spread from friend to friend on social media, but positive posts spread more widely. Study author James Fowler says that researchers should study how to magnify the positive effects of social networks to "create an epidemic of well-being."[20]

> "It turns out that when you talk with a little more depth on Facebook to people you already like, you feel better."[19]
>
> —Robert Kraut, professor of human-computer interaction, Carnegie Mellon University

Meeting New People

Many people use digital media primarily to maintain connections with people they already know in real life. But others go online to seek out a new community and may build new, meaningful friendships. Digital media make it easy for people with similar interests to find each other. People who are into a sport, hobby, game, band, or TV show—no matter how obscure—can easily find each other and bond over their shared interest. In addition, shy people who struggle to connect in real life often feel much more comfortable with online interactions.

On the social site Twitch, people watch streamers playing video games while participating in live chat rooms. Kintinue, a Twitch streamer who prefers to use only her screen name, has built a vibrant online community of fans and friends. She knows people who met and got married through Twitch. She knows other people who once felt depressed and isolated but have come out of their shells after finding a supportive online community. One of her fans credits this online community with helping her overcome social anxiety and giving her the courage to pursue a college education. Kintinue says, "[Twitch] gives you the opportunity to meet people you never would have gotten to meet and see cultures you never would have gotten to experience."[21] One year, an online friend flew to the United States from Qatar to celebrate Kintinue's birthday with her.

Any social site or digital medium that supports an active community of users may help new friends or romantic partners meet each other. People have met future husbands, wives, and best friends through online multiplayer games as well as social media sites such as Facebook or Twitter. Online dating sites and apps make the search for love even more straightforward. "If you're single, and you carry a mobile phone, you basically have a 24/7 singles bar in your pocket,"[22] says Eric Klinenberg, a sociologist at New York University. In both the United Kingdom and the United States, about a third of new relationships begin with online dating. Since 2000, meeting online has become more common for US couples than meeting in college or through family or coworkers. Same-sex couples especially rely on online dating to find partners. Many families today would not exist if not for the Internet and other digital media.

People today have more power than ever before to connect with friends, family, and total strangers. But the same technology that connects people can also isolate them. People may use digital media to disappear from the real world or to build and enhance real-world relationships. They may send out hurtful or insulting messages, or they may support friends with love and affection. Balance is key in making sure social media exerts a positive influence on relationships.

CHAPTER TWO

A Sharing Society

A teen spends her free time altering photos of animals to make them look as if they are playing sports. One day she gets a tweet asking if she sells T-shirts of her pictures. She decides to turn the hobby into a business. In an afternoon, she can build and launch a website or an app and create accounts for the business on all major social media platforms. Within a few weeks, she has the potential to reach a global audience—and she can do all of this for almost no up-front cost at all. If she happens to need money to make her idea a reality, she can collect it through crowdfunding.

Digital media allow businesses instant, easy access to consumers. Consumers in turn have instant, easy access to a huge range of goods and services. They also have the ability to provide public feedback on every transaction. In addition, large networks of people can easily communicate and share resources. As a result, the dynamics of work, the economy, and society are changing. People are exchanging resources and services in a manner that some experts refer to as the sharing economy. They are also going online for education and to organize social movements and revolutions.

A Retail Apocalypse

Many products that used to require physical packaging—such as news, books, movies, and games—now exist almost entirely as digital content. This has drastically reduced their cost and eliminated the need for middlemen, or businesses that help get a product from the creator to the consumer. People increasingly go online to shop for physical goods as well, such as clothing, electronics, and even food. They no longer need to venture out into the real world to shop unless they want to.

The once-popular Toys"R"Us superstore chain was one of 650 retail businesses filing for bankruptcy in 2017. Traditional retail stores have struggled to adapt as more people shop online.

In 2017 over 650 retail businesses failed, a 30 percent increase over the previous year, according to BankruptcyData.com. The failures included former giant Toys"R"Us and the clothing store rue21. Some called the situation a retail apocalypse. Part of the blame falls on Amazon, the giant online retailer. A 2016 report from Consumer Intelligence Research Partners found that around half of US households pay for an Amazon Prime membership. As more people choose to shop on Amazon, fewer customers visit traditional stores. In order to compete, traditional stores must offer a smooth online experience, complete with apps that offer swift ordering from a phone or tablet.

The End of Ownership

In addition, culture itself is changing. Young people today tend to prefer to spend money on travel or restaurants rather than material goods. One possible explanation for this change in behavior is a desire for experiences that can be shared through social media. Traveling and dining out make for better Instagram posts than trips to the mall. Young people are not buying cars and TVs, says Taylor Smith, chief executive officer (CEO) of Blueboard, a company that designs experience packages for businesses. He explains, "[Young people] are renting scooters and touring Vietnam, rocking out at music festivals, or hiking Machu Picchu."[23] They want to do exciting, unusual things—and they want to share these experiences virtually with their social networks.

As a result of this culture shift, ownership is becoming less relevant. For example, private cars were once important status symbols. But today more people are seeing them as a waste of resources. Private cars sit unused in a driveway or parking lot 95 percent of the time, according to *Fortune* magazine. Plus, a person who owns a car has to pay for maintenance, insurance, and taxes. Finally, time spent driving is time that a person cannot—or at least should not—text or check e-mail or social media. So some young people have chosen not to buy a car or even get a license. Car-sharing companies such as Zipcar, Uber, and Lyft allow people to rent cars for quick trips or to share rides. Bike sharing has also become extremely popular in many cities around the world.

The sharing economy does not end with transportation. "Millions of people are sharing not only automobiles and bicycles, but also their homes, clothes, tools, toys, and skills,"[24] says Jeremy Rifkin, an economist and author of *The Zero Marginal Cost Society*. Airbnb and similar companies allow people to rent out their homes or apartments to visitors. Through BonAppetour, popular in Europe and Asia, tourists can pay for a home-cooked meal at a local's house. Rent the Runway is a company that lends designer clothing and accessories to subscribers. Other companies provide the same type of service for jewelry, power tools, and other items. Through Craigslist, Facebook, eBay,

> "Millions of people are sharing not only automobiles and bicycles, but also their homes, clothes, tools, toys, and skills."[24]
>
> —Jeremy Rifkin, economist and author of *The Zero Marginal Cost Society*

and similar sites, people can easily find someone to buy or take away items they no longer need.

When it comes to music, movies, and TV shows, services such as Spotify, Netflix, and Hulu offer subscriber-based access. Many people no longer gather personal collections of music, movies, or books. They just borrow or rent the entertainment they want when they want it. Rifkin predicts that they very idea of ownership will come to seem old-fashioned in the near future.

The Importance of Trust

The sharing economy only works when people trust each other. But it is human nature not to trust strangers. "There are psychological studies up the wazoo about how we mistrust people when we don't know them,"[25] says Charles Green, CEO of Trusted Advisor Associates, a company that advises businesses on how to build trust. Cindy Manit, a Lyft driver in San Francisco, says that some of her friends and family think letting strangers into her car seems like a creepy thing to do. But she disagrees. "It's not just some person off the street," she says. Lyft and other companies that facilitate similar transactions have made it a priority to help the sellers and buyers get to know each other. "We don't mess with people we know,"[26] says Green.

Lyft riders must link a Facebook profile or phone number to their account. In addition, drivers and riders rate each other. Airbnb hosts include photos of themselves on their listings, and the site encourages communication between hosts and guests. Turo, a car-sharing service that allows people to rent and drive other people's cars, requires that owners hand off the keys and vehicle in person. CEO Andre Haddad says that this brief exchange encourages customers to take better care of the cars. "People strike up a conversation and realize they have something in common, which boosts trust and makes people feel accountable," says Haddad. "They're going to have to return this car to that person and look them in the eye."[27]

Odd Jobs

People who want to earn a little extra money these days have an interesting option. They can make themselves available to do odd jobs for other people through a site such as TaskRabbit, Handy, or Thumbtack. Mostly, people visit these sites to find someone to help with fix-it jobs around the house, cleaning, moving, or personal assistance. But some jobs are more unusual.

Sam Ridley was hired to spend two hours playing with a tiny Chihuahua while the dog's owner got her costume ready for a dance show. Aisha Russell once arrived to clean an apartment in New York City and discovered a pet pig. She also regularly chops up vegetables for a family. She says that everyone sometimes has a task that they don't feel like doing. "They are now able to hire someone at a reasonable rate," she says.

Quoted in Andrea Kramar, "Some of the Strangest Jobs People Have Paid Others to Do on TaskRabbit," CNBC, January 17, 2017. www.cnbc.com.

A good experience on Lyft, Airbnb, Turo, or another sharing platform leads to good ratings and reviews, meaning that others will know that the person is trustworthy. Ratings and the online reputations they support matter immensely in the sharing economy. On most sharing platforms, a bad rating can significantly hurt that user's business or even end it completely. For example, if an Uber driver's rating falls too low, the person will not be allowed to drive anymore. That driver's customers wield a huge amount of power, often without even realizing it.

The Power of Reputation

This customer power extends to many other products and services. Shoppers can sort products on Amazon and other online stores by ratings. They can view reviews that sometimes contain pictures or video to help decide whether a product seems worth purchasing. Reviews also come in handy when choosing a travel destination or deciding where to eat, where to get a haircut, or whom to hire for a home project. Sites and apps such as Yelp, TripAdvisor, and Angie's List contain hundreds of millions of reviews of hotels, restaurants, bars, stores, spas, plumbers, carpenters, and more.

People have become so dependent on reviews to make decisions that even a bad review is better than no review at all. On Amazon, products rated with one star sell better than those with no stars, according to the company. Reviews also tend to matter more than the price of the item, meaning that many shoppers are more likely to buy the item with the best reviews even if it is more expensive than the alternative. "Reputation is everything, and if we cannot crowdsource it or quantify something instantly, it doesn't exist,"[28] writes Tomas Chamorro-Premuzic in an article for the *Guardian*.

Sites and apps such as Yelp contain hundreds of millions of reviews of hotels, restaurants, plumbers, and almost any other product or service. These reviews have a significant impact on consumer choices.

Online reputation comes in many forms, from starred ratings and reviews of contractors, products, or services to recommendations on LinkedIn, views on YouTube, or followers on Facebook, Twitter, or Instagram. These reputation systems are so important to the success of a product or business that companies go to great lengths to increase and improve their numbers. Amazon has a program in place to supply select customers with free products in return for reviews. These customers receive the item and may rate it however they wish. In other cases, however, companies have paid for five-star reviews or social media followers. In especially devious cases, a company may even purchase one-star reviews of its competitors. Sometimes, paid reviewers or followers are real people, but not always. Software exists that can write fairly convincing reviews or create numerous fake social media accounts. For these reasons, online ratings are not always trustworthy.

The Trouble with Ratings

The ratings system has other downsides. Real customers may not use their power fairly. An Uber or Lyft rider may dock stars on a driver's rating for bad traffic, refusing to speed, or talking too much or too little. As a result, drivers often feel as if they must work very hard to put on a five-star performance. "Ratings create strong incentives for drivers to be subservient, to smile, to be happy even when they're not,"[29] says Brishen Rogers, a law professor at Temple University. Traditional taxi drivers, who are not publicly rated, are free to act grouchy.

> "Ratings create strong incentives for drivers to be subservient, to smile, to be happy even when they're not."[29]
>
> —Brishen Rogers, law professor, Temple University

In addition, online ratings systems and the sharing economy in general support discrimination against groups of people. Most sharing apps require users to sign up with their real names and photos or link to Facebook profiles to help build trust. But when a name or photo belongs to someone from a marginalized group, stereotypes and biases come into play. Dennis Zhang, a business researcher at Washington University in St. Louis, sent hundreds of requests to Airbnb hosts in three cities. Each request was exactly the same except for the name of the guest—for example, Laquisha or Emily. "The accounts with distinct African-American names are 18 percent less likely to be accepted compared to accounts with distinctly white names,"[30] says Zhang.

Dyne Suh experienced this sort of discrimination in person when an Airbnb host canceled her reservation at the last minute. The host made racist remarks indicating that Suh was not welcome because she was Asian. Airbnb kicked that host off the site. The company has also committed to reducing discrimination. But racism, sexism, and other forms of exclusion will likely continue to flourish on many sharing platforms.

Of course, people have long discriminated against each other and have always relied on reputation to make purchasing decisions. However, digital media increases the reach of people's opinions in both time and space. A word-of-mouth warning against a business reaches only a few close friends and may soon be forgotten. But one bad review online could potentially reach an audience of millions and last for years.

The Long Tail and the Superstar

This ability to reach the entire world with digital content has drastically changed the potential reach of every single person's ideas. But at the same time, every single idea must also compete against a dizzying array of other choices. In the past, transportation costs and production limitations made it so authors, musicians, movie producers, comedians, and other entertainers could only reach a limited audience. In addition, business and service providers could usually only serve a small geographical area.

Today almost all entertainment content has gone digital, and many businesses and services also exist entirely as apps. These products are so easily replicated and distributed that one artist or developer can easily reach the entire world. Authors self-publish books through Amazon, musicians or entertainers post videos on YouTube, and game or app developers sell their products through online marketplaces such as Steam, the iTunes App Store, or Google Play. Craftspeople or collectors who produce or deal in physical objects market themselves on Etsy or eBay. All kinds of entrepreneurs use Kickstarter, GoFundMe, Indiegogo, or similar sites to raise money for a new business or product idea. Artists and entrepreneurs of all kinds have gained independence and flexibility, but they have lost out on the stability and support that sponsors such as record labels and publishers used to provide.

With so many products competing for customer attention, two things happen. One is that very small niche markets can flourish. This is also called the long tail. Products that once could not find enough customers when limited to a geographic area can now find buyers in the much larger and more diverse digital landscape.

Exploding Kittens

The most successful Kickstarter project of all time describes itself in the following way: "This is a card game for people who are into kittens and explosions and laser beams and sometimes goats." The game, titled Exploding Kittens, raised $8.8 million from almost 220,000 backers. A group of friends created the game. Elan Lee and Shane Small are both game designers, and Matthew Inman is the artist behind the popular online cartoon *The Oatmeal*. They had originally hoped to raise $10,000 and pack up around five hundred orders in their garage over a weekend. But the incredible success of the campaign quickly changed that plan and turned their weekend project into a major international business. Lee had previously founded four other companies, but this was his first Kickstarter campaign. "It's the most exciting and terrifying new company I've ever started," he says.

Quoted in Amy Feldman, "Ten of the Most Successful Companies Built on Kickstarter," *Forbes*, April 14, 2016. www.forbes.com.

For example, podcasts on obscure topics can find enough listeners willing to support their channels. The second effect is that one superstar may completely dominate an industry. That person or business may make millions or even billions while every other competitor struggles or fails. For example, if one mapping app offers better features than another, then almost no one will buy competing apps. A person only needs one mapping app. When all customers have access to the very best, they are unlikely to purchase lower-quality products.

Education for All

In addition to sharing material goods and services, people today can also easily share information and ideas. Thanks to the Internet, education on a huge range of topics is now freely or cheaply available to everyone with a connection. Blog posts, articles, and videos that offer training on a variety of topics have been around since the early days of the Internet. But in 2011 one online class changed the course of higher education. Sebastian Thrun, an artificial intelligence (AI) researcher best known for his work on self-driving cars, was preparing to teach an introductory course on AI to a group of around two hundred students at Stanford University. Inspired by a talk he had seen about the potential of online education, Thrun decided to make the course available online for free.

Thrun thought he might get a few thousand students. But the numbers kept climbing and climbing. By the time the course began, 160,000 students from countries all around the world had enrolled. And 23,000 of those students completed the class. Brian Guan, a forty-four-year-old software engineer who lives in Palo Alto, California, was among those who finished. In 2012 he said, "I wish that the always-available, always-replayable and free nature of this style of learning can help to elevate education . . . for all of human kind."[31]

Guan seems to be getting his wish. Thrun founded the website Udacity, which offers online courses on a range of topics. His goal is to make quality education available to everyone around the world, including poor people in developing countries who would otherwise never have access to top institutions. A number of competing companies, including Coursera, now offer massive open online courses, or MOOCs for short. For many people, the old model of an education that ends after high school or college no longer makes sense. Due to the incredible pace at which new technology is developed, most people must learn new skills throughout their lives.

Networked Revolutions

People are also gathering online to organize for social change. In 2011 a wave of protests and revolutions now called the Arab Spring swept through North Africa and the Middle East. In Tunisia, Egypt, Libya, and Yemen, protestors eventually overthrew the ruling regime. In Syria the revolution sparked a civil war that was still raging in 2018. In each of these uprisings, protestors used social media to organize and also to broadcast what was happening. Wael Ghonim, an activist who helped lead anti-government

Social change and activism have been propelled by the communication power of social media. Like other recent social movements, the Black Lives Matter movement has spread its message through social media.

protests in Egypt, said, "Without Facebook, without Twitter, without Google, without You Tube, [the revolution] would have never happened."[32]

Activists have also used social media to spread awareness or raise money in the wake of a tragedy. In 2014 terrorists kidnapped a group of 276 high school girls in the middle of the night from their dormitory in northern Nigeria. Activists took to social media, tagging posts with the hashtag #BringBackOurGirls. All around the world, people lamented the girls' plight. In 2016 twenty-one of the girls returned to their families, and in 2017 another eighty-two were freed, partially thanks to all the international attention.

> "Without Facebook, without Twitter, without Google, without You Tube, [the revolution] would have never happened."[32]
>
> —Wael Ghonim, activist during the 2011 Egyptian revolution

In the United States the Black Lives Matter movement has been going strong since 2013. The movement calls attention to the deaths of innocent black people at the hands of police officers and tries to prevent similar tragedies in the future. Participants use the hashtag #blacklivesmatter. In 2017 two huge marches took place, a Climate March and the Women's March. Both emerged as ideas on social media and rapidly grew into real events. Similarly, in late 2017 and early 2018, the #metoo movement gained momentum among women who had experienced sexual harassment or assault. Numerous men in power lost their jobs after victims who had remained silent finally found the courage to speak up.

Digital media gives everyone a voice. Plus, people with similar interests and ideas can easily find each other and join their voices into a shout. Any person—a business owner, a singer, a young woman, or a group of resistance fighters—can get up on a digital stage and speak to the rest of the world.

CHAPTER THREE

Information Overload

An elderly woman wants to know what time the soccer game is starting. A young man is trying to recall who wrote a book that he really enjoyed reading. A child wonders how long it would take to travel to the moon. All three can get answers to their questions in a matter of seconds—all they have to do is *google* it. This act of looking up information has become so important to human culture that the American Dialect Society named *google* the word of the decade in 2010.

Google and other search engines faithfully churn out a list of good answers to just about any question. "Google is an astonishing boon to humanity, gathering up and concentrating information and ideas that were once scattered so broadly around the world that hardly anyone could profit from them,"[33] says Heather Pringle, a writer at *Archaeology* magazine. The Internet offers a treasure trove of information, and a search engine is the key to getting inside.

Big Data

The world's knowledge is growing at an unprecedented rate, thanks to the increasing capacity of digital technology to generate and store data. The Google Books Library Project aimed to digitize all the world's physical books and has scanned an estimated 30 million titles. Most newspapers, magazines, and scientific journals publish primarily online. *Wikipedia* offers crowdsourced encyclopedia entries on any topic. Every single e-mail, search query, digital photo, video, and tweet adds to the pile of data. In 2016, for every minute of every day, YouTube users shared four hundred hours of new video, according to Domo, a digital technology

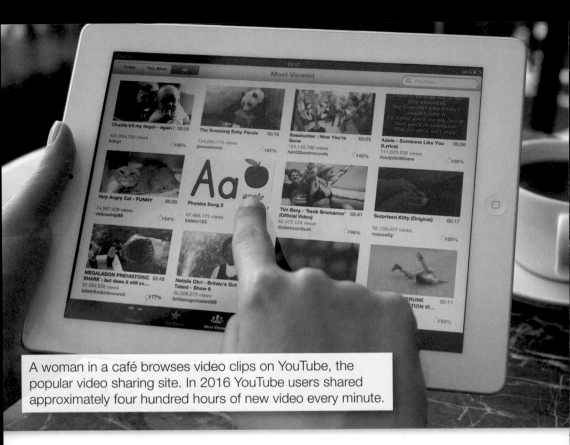

A woman in a café browses video clips on YouTube, the popular video sharing site. In 2016 YouTube users shared approximately four hundred hours of new video every minute.

consulting firm. And people are not the only ones continuously creating information. Machines also spew out data, including automated logs of computer activity, satellite and sensor measurements, location coordinates, and more. All of this feeds into a phenomenon that experts call "big data."

Big data is really humongous. In just two years in the 2010s, the world produced more new data than during the rest of human history, according to the independent research organization SINTEF. If all the world's data were burned onto CDs, the discs would form five stacks that each reach all the way to the moon. Even taking into account every book, film, and newspaper, physical media makes up just 2 percent of all the world's information, according to *Foreign Affairs*. The rest is all digital.

Cybercrime

Big data has incredible potential to help society, but the phenomenon has its dark side. People post their locations, friendships, photos, personal communications, and more online because sharing makes their lives more enjoyable and convenient. However, sharing all that personal information also puts people at risk. Companies go to great lengths to safeguard digital information, but criminals always find ways to exploit cybersecurity systems. They spread viruses and malware that mess up people's devices. They get a hold of company databases and demand ransom money in exchange. They steal passwords and credit card numbers in order to use people's accounts without permission. They pose as friends, family, banks, or the government and entice people into fraudulent schemes. As the data in the world increases, so does the risk of that data getting misused.

Scandals surrounding personal data abound. In 2017 hackers broke into credit reporting company Equifax's databases. The criminals had access to over 100 million Americans' names, social security numbers, birthdates, addresses, driver's license numbers, as well as some credit card numbers and tax identification numbers. That same year, Yahoo! revealed that during a 2013 attack, hackers had access to all 3 billion of its users' account information, making this the largest hack ever.

Knowledge Is Power

Criminals are not the only ones mistreating people's information. Any large organization, from a private company to a government, may use data to control people or perform surveillance. This could lead to breaches of personal freedom and privacy. Today the world collects an unprecedented amount of knowledge, which translates into a huge amount of power just waiting for someone to wield it.

In China an app called Alipay has almost entirely replaced credit cards and paper currency. Many people use the app to pay for everything, from meals and parking to doctor's appointments, airline tickets, and car insurance. The app stores all of this information. Ant Financial, the company that owns the app, uses this information to give each user a credit score. A credit score is most often used to decide whether a person is trustworthy enough to borrow money. But Ant Financial seems to be planning to turn this score into something bigger. It could soon become a kind of social score that determines if someone is a good or bad member of society. The company's chief executive, Lucy Peng, said that the score "will ensure that the bad people in society don't have a place to go, while good people can move freely and without obstruction."[34] Someone with a bad score in a system like this could potentially end up blocked from making purchases, voting, or otherwise participating in society.

In the United States the government regularly intercepts phone and e-mail communications in the name of national security. In 2013 Edward Snowden, a former analyst at the CIA, leaked information that the National Security Agency (NSA) had been collecting records on tens of millions of Americans' phone calls without their permission or knowledge. The organization knew the locations and times of calls, as well as which numbers called each other and how long each call lasted. In addition, Snowden revealed extensive spying on other countries around the world, including America's allies.

Snowden had to go into hiding after the leak, leaving behind a comfortable salary, stable career, and family he loves. He said, "I'm willing to sacrifice all of that because I can't in good conscience allow the US government to destroy privacy, internet freedom, and basic liberties for people around the world with this massive surveillance machine they're secretly building."[35] Some called Snowden a traitor for exposing his country's secrets. But others revered him as a hero for standing up for people's freedom. Despite the leak, the surveillance continues. In 2018 US president Donald Trump signed a bill that renewed the NSA's program.

Propaganda and Censorship

Misusing or over-collecting information is just one part of the problem. Corporations and governments may also limit or control people's access to information. Since ancient times, world leaders have controlled news and other information in order to make themselves look good. They may deliberately spread messages that support their ideas, called propaganda, or they may prevent messages they do not agree with from reaching an audience, called censorship. During the twentieth century, socialist governments in Russia and China maintained a strong grip over the media that their people consumed.

Digital media has helped loosen this grip. It is not easy to stop the flow of information online. Today China continues to delete sensitive posts and maintain firewalls that prevent access to parts of the Internet. However, "anybody with some internet savvy can probably go over the 'Great Firewall' to access whatever they want,"[36] says Jie Li, who studies the media culture in China at Harvard University. In North Korea, however, the ruling regime has taken censorship to an extreme. People there have almost no access to the Internet or to the outside world in general. Even Western movies are banned. North Koreans may only consume news and entertainment that the government provides.

A student in North Korea uses a computer terminal. North Koreans have almost no access to the Internet and are only able to view sites and information that their government provides.

For now, most citizens of democratic countries have free and equal access to all of the information on the Internet. However, in the United States, this equal access may soon change. In 2017 the Federal Communications Commission (FCC) voted to get rid of net neutrality laws. Without these laws in place, companies would be free to charge fees to users to unlock access to certain websites. Some people are concerned that Internet providers could misuse their power under the new rules in order to restrict access to content they disagree with. Overwhelmingly, people in the United States want the Internet to remain free and open. "An open internet is critical for new ideas and economic opportunity—and internet providers shouldn't be able to decide what people can see online or charge more for certain websites,"[37] says Sheryl Sandberg, chief operating officer of Facebook. In 2018 Washington became the first state to respond to the FCC's decision with its own law making it illegal for Internet providers to block or slow down access to online content.

Fake News

Although digital technology makes censorship more difficult, it also makes propaganda easier than ever to spread. Online media can quickly reach millions or even billions of people, and many people keep a digital device nearby at all times. Those with power and influence can use this enhanced reach to spread whatever messages they want people to hear. If one powerful person manages to inspire trust in his or her messages and mistrust in everyone else's, then followers will not believe dissenting messages, even if they are based on factual evidence.

Today many US politicians label any information they dislike as "fake news." Trump has used the term more than sixty times on Twitter, usually to discredit reporting that questions his decisions or leadership. When the term first emerged in 2016, a reporter used it to describe made-up news reports. Compelling, fabricated stories were being disguised as real news and shared on Facebook. The authors of some of these stories most likely

How to Put News to the Test

It can be tricky to tell real news from fake. Taking just a few minutes to ask some questions about a story can help determine if it is a good idea to trust the information.

1. Does the story seem ridiculous?
   If a story seems completely crazy or too good to be true, it probably is.

2. Check the author.
   Who wrote the story? Is the author even a real person? Search for the name online to quickly check how much experience the author has with the topic.

3. Check the site.
   Investigate the site or organization hosting the story. Does it have a mission that might skew its reporting? Does it employ editors and fact-checkers? These experts review every story at major news organizations such as the *New York Times* and the *Wall Street Journal*. A thorough editorial process makes stories more trustworthy.

4. Look for an original source.
   Many news sites simply rewrite stories from other sources. Follow links in the story to find the organization or researchers that originated the news.

5. Ask an expert.
   Bring the story to a librarian or teacher. Does this person believe it?

just wanted to get rich. They wanted the links to spread quickly through Facebook and other social media, generating lots of online advertising money.

However, other fake stories had ulterior motives. The US presidential election between Donald Trump and Hillary Clinton was a hot topic at the time. One made-up story said that Clinton was abusing children in the basement of a Washington, DC, pizza restaurant. The story, now nicknamed Pizzagate, spread through right-wing media even though it was a complete lie. Eventually, a man armed himself and drove to the restaurant to try to rescue the children. Of course they were not there. In fact, the restaurant didn't even have a basement. No one got hurt, and the man was arrested. After Clinton lost the election, she talked in a speech about "the epidemic of malicious fake news and false propaganda that flooded social media." She went on to say, "It's now clear that so-called fake news can have real-world consequences."[38] Pizzagate was one consequence. In addition, evidence has since come to light that Russia intentionally spread misinformation on Facebook in an attempt to sway the US election in Trump's favor. Fake news may have influenced the outcome.

> "It's now clear that so-called fake news can have real-world consequences."[38]
>
> —Hillary Clinton, former US secretary of state and 2016 Democratic Party candidate for president

The End of Truth

There are two problems associated with the fake news phenomenon. The first is when people believe in fake news, like the Pizzagate story, and the second is when people refuse to believe in real news. AI software now makes it possible to produce a doctored video or audio file of a powerful person saying something he or she never actually said, while realistic photo editing has been around for years. "You don't need to create the fake video for this tech to have a serious impact,"[39] says Renee DiResta, an expert in disinformation campaigns. Just pointing out that it is possible to make fake videos casts doubt on real videos. For example, a real video exists in which Trump, before he was president, made vulgar remarks about women. Later, Trump said, "We don't think that was my voice,"[40] implying that someone may have faked the video. "What happens when anyone

> "What happens when anyone can make it appear as if anything has happened, regardless of whether or not it did?"[41]
>
> —Aviv Ovadya, chief technologist at the Center for Social Media Responsibility

can make it appear as if anything has happened, regardless of whether or not it did?"[41] asks Aviv Ovadya, chief technologist at the Center for Social Media Responsibility.

Today society is facing a truth crisis. When someone like Trump labels a story "fake news," he is signaling to his followers that they should not trust that story or its source. When it comes to spreading fake news, most politicians, social groups, and religious leaders do not have to fabricate false stories. They simply cast doubt on factual stories with which they disagree. For example, a large number of people around the world either do not believe that the planet's climate is changing or believe that this change is not a serious problem. To help spread this false belief, climate change deniers suggest that scientists have ulterior

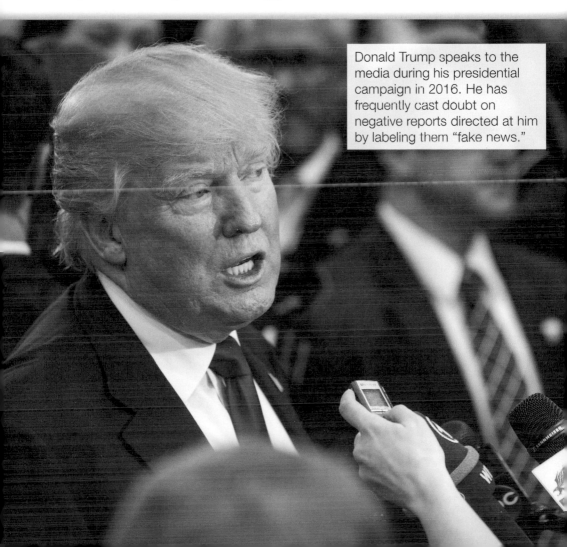

Donald Trump speaks to the media during his presidential campaign in 2016. He has frequently cast doubt on negative reports directed at him by labeling them "fake news."

motives. This makes their results seem less truthful. As a result, some countries may not put policies in place to help keep climate change under control.

Key facts about the world once formed a common ground that everyone could stand on when discussing controversial issues. Today this common ground is eroding. People are increasingly suspicious of scientists, professors, doctors, and others who have traditionally been regarded as experts. Isaac Asimov, a famous science fiction writer, warned of what he called a "cult of ignorance" in the United States. He explained the phenomenon as a belief that "my ignorance is just as good as your knowledge."[42] People whose ideas are not backed by facts assume that their views are just as valid as those who have done actual research.

Going Viral

Most online media reach a relatively small audience. But every once in a while, something goes viral. A huge number of people share the same content all within a short time frame. Most viral posts are funny or ridiculous. Others tug at the emotions, good or bad. For example, in the summer of 2014, an estimated 17 million people dumped buckets of ice over their heads to help raise money and awareness for a charity that supports research into the disease amyotrophic lateral sclerosis. Meanwhile, in 2018 a college student posted a series of racist rants on Instagram. When the videos went public, she experienced a huge backlash and was expelled from school.

Finally, some viral content offers breaking news. In 2011, when a team of US Navy SEALs killed terrorist Osama bin Laden, a tweet about what had happened went viral before the president could address the nation. Unfortunately, tweets about fake news tend to spread more widely and more quickly than those about true news, according to a 2018 study in *Science*. "If something sounds crazy stupid you wouldn't think it would get that much traction," says Alex Kasprak, a journalist at the fact-checking website Snopes. "But those are the ones that go massively viral."

Quoted in Katie Langin, "Fake News Spreads Faster Than True News on Twitter—Thanks to People, Not Bots," *Science*, March 8, 2018. www.sciencemag.org.

The ease of putting up websites and online content makes it so that anyone anywhere can claim to be an expert. "Truth is no longer dictated by authorities, but is networked by peers,"[43] says Kevin Kelly, cofounder of *Wired* magazine. People are continuously bombarded with information from a variety of sources, including major news organizations and scientific experts as well as political parties, religious organizations, scientists, family, friends, and celebrities. Facts, opinions, and propaganda jumble together on a person's Facebook wall or Twitter feed. Important news about the world almost always breaks first through Twitter or another social platform. Kelly continues, "For every fact there is a counterfact and all these counterfacts and facts look identical online, which is confusing to most people."[44]

> "A wealth of information creates a poverty of attention."[45]
>
> —Herbert Simon, winner of the 1978 Nobel Prize in Economics

Researchers at Stanford University looked into this confusion. In 2016 they asked middle school, high school, and college students to judge the credibility of a variety of online information sources. Most of the students failed miserably. They could not tell activist groups from neutral ones or paid stories from standard news. Eighty percent of the students thought a story labeled "sponsored content" was reliable news. In fact, the story was an advertisement. The study showed that most young people today do not have the skills or the patience to verify online information. As a result, they end up believing falsehoods and doubting truths.

Shallow Thoughts

The excess of information that digital media makes available does not tend to educate people. Rather, it overwhelms them. "A wealth of information creates a poverty of attention,"[45] said Herbert Simon, winner of the 1978 Nobel Prize in Economics. People today must divide their attention among too many different information sources. As a result, people spend less time consuming each piece of media. They rarely read entire books, articles, or web pages. Instead, they skim and skip around, stopping briefly only on the most relevant or appealing content.

This method of information gathering seems to be changing how people's brains work. Since they no longer focus for a long time on one thing, deep thinking may become more difficult in general. Nicholas Carr, author of *The Shallows: What the Internet Is Doing to Our Brains*, explains how the change feels to him: "Once I was a scuba diver in the sea of words. Now I zip along the surface like a guy on a jet ski."[46]

People also no longer have to remember phone numbers, directions, or basic facts about the world. They can outsource that brain space to Google. In a 2016 study, neuroscientists Ryota Kanai and Kep-Kee Loh looked at how Internet usage has shaped the way people think. They write, "In terms of information processing, we are shifting toward a shallow mode of learning characterized by quick scanning, reduced contemplation, and memory consolidation."[47] However, this change is not necessarily a bad thing, so long as people use the freed-up space for more creative and critical thinking.

Emotions and Belief

People also deal with the overflow of information by selecting organizations and personalities that they like to hear from and ignoring everything else. They choose whom to follow on social media or sign up for e-mail news or alerts from specific websites. Typically, the news sources people choose support their existing beliefs. This creates echo chambers of people who share a belief system. For example, those who deny climate change tend to only hear from each other. Meanwhile, those who are trying to combat climate change also talk among themselves. This creates feedback loops in which the more people hear from those with similar views, the more firmly entrenched those views get.

It does not matter how many facts about climate change the scientists find. Those who deny it exists will likely never read these facts—and if they do, they will not believe them. George Lakoff, a philosopher at the University of California–Berkeley, points out that many people share a misconception about facts. They believe that "the truth will set us free,"[48] he says. They think that telling people facts will lead them to the right conclusions, because people make rational decisions. In fact, emotions rule decision making. People who have suffered brain damage that impairs emotions may still have a very strong intellect, but they cannot make simple decisions. Even when a person thinks he or she is making a logical or informed choice, emotions sway the final decision.

In some ways, digital media and big data make people smarter than ever before. Everyone has instant access to all the world's information. But in other ways, the information overload makes people less intelligent. They spend less time with each piece of content, rarely seek out all the different sides of an issue, and have difficulty determining which information is most trustworthy. The truth is out there online, but it is hidden among an avalanche of half-truths, lies, and funny cat videos.

CHAPTER FOUR

Identity Dilemma

Thanks to the cascade of information available online, people can instantly find out about almost anything in the world. This ability has a flip side, though. The world can easily find out everything about an individual and can contact him or her at any time. A digitally connected person is never truly anonymous or out of touch.

Most people willingly accept public exposure in exchange for convenience and connection. They happily share their lives on social media. Teens regularly post selfies and tag them with a location. People of all ages share many of their deepest hopes and fears in text messages, online comments, and public blogs.

All of these messages craft a person's social identity, or how the outside world views him or her. Inside, each person also has a personal identity, or how that person views himself or herself. People seem to have a lot of control over their social identities online, since they choose what to disclose about themselves. However, they have no control over what other people share or say about them. And all of this content has the potential to live forever on the Internet.

A Selfie Society

In the early days of the Internet, many users remained anonymous. They used nicknames or funny phrases instead of their real names. This usually meant their offline identity remained distinct from one or many online identities. This trend continues in some areas, including some online games. However, most online services today, including Facebook, require real names. People increasingly use their real identities in all online activities. They may not differentiate between a public and private self.

Some may even feel like they would cease to exist if they lost all of the photos, profiles, and other data making up their digital identity.

Selfies are a new form of self-expression perfectly adapted to the digital age. The #selfie tag seems to have first emerged on the photo-sharing site Flickr in 2004, but selfies took off when cell phones with front-facing cameras were introduced in 2010. "[Selfies are] about presenting yourself in the best way . . . [similar to] when women put on makeup or men who bodybuild to look a certain way,"[49] says Mariann Hardey, a lecturer in marketing at Durham University in the United Kingdom. People love attention, and that is what a selfie attracts. Rebecca Brown, a twenty-three-year-old graduate student from the United Kingdom, says that she usually posts a selfie before she goes out with friends. "If people start liking your selfie, then obviously you're going to get a natural buzz. It gives you a nice boost and you can walk with that little bit more confidence,"[50] says Brown.

Selfies are a new form of self-expression perfectly adapted to the digital age. They took off when cell phones with front-facing cameras were introduced in 2010.

Many experts have expressed concern that selfies may indicate that people are becoming more self-centered. Others worry about the fact that many young people try to catch others' attention with sexy or suggestive selfies. Yet the people who share selfies see a positive side. Many people post selfies to better understand themselves or to remember key moments of their lives. Brown says, "It's almost like a visual diary. I can look back and see what I looked like at a particular time, what I was wearing. It's exploring your identity in digital form. . . . A selfie is a format and a platform to share who you are."[51]

> "A selfie is a format and a platform to share who you are."[51]
>
> —Rebecca Brown, twenty-three-year-old graduate student

Discovering Who You Are

Selfies and other forms of social sharing do more than just broadcast a person's identity. They also help develop and craft that identity. Children and teens are still discovering who they want to be as adults. Experimenting with new identities is part of that process. In the real world, a teen may listen to new music, change hairstyles, or wear different clothing. The virtual world offers many more options for experimentation, including the possibility of trying on several completely different identities simultaneously. For example, a teen boy may play the part of a silly jokester in an online game while posting dark, moody images on Instagram. In a 2011 survey, the British charity Kidscape found that kids begin to try out new identities online as early as age eleven.

Often, teens' online experimentation involves telling small lies or stretching the truth. The same survey found that half of the preteens and teens lie about personal details online. Most often they lie about their age. But they also lie in an effort to seem smarter, more good-looking, more popular, or wealthier. For example, a young boy from a low-income family may brag online about material things that he does not actually own. "It's not so much about who they are but how they want other kids to perceive them,"[52] says University of Texas–Austin professor S. Craig Watkins, who studies young people's digital behavior.

If young people take experimentation too far or reach too wide of an audience, the results may haunt them for the rest of their lives. The act of sexting, or sending nude photos or sexual videos via text message, is an alarming trend that many young people have participated in. It is illegal in the United States for those under age eighteen to send or receive these types of images. And even if the exchange seems private, any digital image could become public very easily. "Most young people are extremely likely to create something online akin to a tattoo—something they cannot remove later in life, even if desired, without great difficulty,"[53] write John Palfrey and Urs Gasser, authors of *Born Digital*. The "tattoo" may be an embarrassing or revealing photo or video; participation in a fan site about a show, band, or celebrity that later becomes unpopular; or even a racist, sexist, or hateful comment. Digital mistakes are nearly impossible to scrub away.

People Are the Product

Each person broadcasts information important to his or her own identity in an effort to gain social acceptance and status. Social media companies allow users to join for free, encourage sharing, and promote their platforms as helping connect the world. But this is not charity work. Facebook, Twitter, YouTube, and other social platforms are selling a product. The people who use the platform *are* that product. Their interactions are gold to advertisers, who analyze social content to help target advertising.

Every piece of content a user shares does not really belong to that person. It belongs to the company facilitating the sharing. Even people who understand this tend to believe that only

Catfishing

Most people use their real names online. But it is still fairly easy to use digital technology to hide behind a false identity. A 2010 documentary titled *Catfish* told the true story of Nev Schulman, a young man who received a painting in the mail from an eight-year-old artist. He then started talking to the girl's older sister, Megan, and fell in love with her. But when he traveled from New York to Michigan to meet her, things started to unravel. Megan never existed. The eight-year-old girl never made any paintings. The artist was the girl's mother, Angela. She had created fake Facebook profiles for Megan as well as a circle of friends.

The term *catfish* has since become slang for a person who pretends to be someone else in order to lure a person into an online relationship. In the best-case scenario, this leads only to embarrassment and heartbreak. In the worst-case scenario, online predators create fake profiles to lure victims. When arranging a real-life meeting with an online friend, it is extremely important to have the meeting in a public place and to tell someone about it, just in case something goes wrong.

information they choose to share will end up associated with their profile. If they are careful, they can keep certain relationships or personal details private. This is often not the case. Facebook collects information about its users from what other users share, including e-mail address books and phone contact lists.

For example, a psychiatrist deliberately chose not to friend any of her patients or share any of her e-mail or phone contacts on Facebook. But then one of her patients showed her a list of Facebook friend recommendations. "He laughed and said, 'I don't know any of these people who showed up on my list—I'm guessing they see you,'"[54] says the psychiatrist, who chose not to use her name. Indeed, some of the names were other patients'.

This breach of her patients' privacy alarmed the psychiatrist. A journalist helped her investigate what might have happened. It turned out that the psychiatrist had shared her cell phone number on Facebook. Some of her patients likely allowed Facebook access to their phone contacts, which included her number. So Facebook could link the psychiatrist to her patients, even though they were not Facebook friends. "It's a massive privacy fail,"[55] she says. In some cases this sort of breach of privacy could be extremely dangerous. For example, a woman who is trying to escape an abusive relationship may accidentally reveal her contact information or location to her abuser.

In 2018 Facebook's privacy problems became big news. A scandal broke revealing that during the 2016 US presidential race, the Trump campaign managed to gain access to the personal data of 50 million Facebook users. The breach began with a researcher who made an online quiz. People who took the quiz exposed their own data as well as friends' data. Facebook had rules against selling or sharing data accessed this way, but the people involved ignored those rules. Mark Zuckerberg, CEO of Facebook, publicly apologized for what happened. "This was a breach of trust and I'm sorry we didn't do more at the time." [56]

The End of Privacy

The right to privacy is the right to remain anonymous or undisturbed. Digital technology is making it ever easier both to identify people and to disturb them. "What we have thought of as privacy is dying, if not already dead,"[57] write Andrew Burt and Dan Geer in the *New York Times*. Some experts have argued that people today no longer care about privacy because they willingly give out so much information about themselves. When signing up for a new service, most people simply check the box next to the privacy policy or user agreement without reading any of it.

> "What we have thought of as privacy is dying, if not already dead."[57]
>
> —Andrew Burt and Dan Geer, journalists at the *New York Times*

Marketers argue that people give up personal information as a fair trade for store discounts, the free use of certain apps, and

Many Internet users today freely post private pictures and details about themselves. Marketers argue that people give up personal information as a fair trade for free use of apps or store discounts.

more. However, a 2015 survey by the Annenberg School for Communication at the University of Pennsylvania found that the majority of people think these practices are unfair. They do not like giving up personal information, but they need to use digital services to conduct their lives. Some people are trying to make it harder for companies to secretly or stealthily gather data on customers. In California, lawmakers have introduced the Right to Know Act. If it becomes law, companies in California would have to reveal to their users all personal information they collect and store.

The Right to Be Forgotten

Companies are not the only ones invading people's privacy. On social media it is all too easy for a friend or family member to say something or share something that embarrasses, angers, or shames someone else. Facebook does allow its users to untag themselves in photos or flag inappropriate content for removal, but often by the time content has been taken down, it is already too late—too many people already saw it or copied it. Often the damage is accidental, as when a family member reveals a pregnancy before the parents-to-be were ready for the world to know. Other times people say things or share things out of anger to try to hurt someone else. In real life, such an outburst fades with time. But online, this content lives on.

Some people have argued that individuals should have the right to remove data about themselves from the public sphere. If Google associates embarrassing or stigmatizing content with a person, he or she may have trouble finding a job, making friends, or going on dates. In 2014 the European Court of Justice ruled that Europeans have the right to request that material be removed from Google search results if the information is inaccurate or no longer relevant. According to a 2015 survey by Benenson Strategy Group, 88 percent of Americans would support a similar law. Though a right-to-be-forgotten law may protect privacy, it could also potentially be misused to rewrite past history. For example, in 2018 a businessman in England was trying to use the new law to erase mentions of a past criminal conviction. The court must judge if public interest outweighs the right to privacy in this case.

Always On, Always Available

In addition to exposing personal information online, people who use digital technology also regularly give up personal time and space. Being able to contact friends, family, and coworkers from anywhere at any time feels wonderfully convenient. But gaining the ability to reach out to others means losing the ability to remain undisturbed. People who are digitally connected are always on and always available.

Before the digital revolution, when a person left work and went home, it was not polite for that person's coworkers or boss to try to contact him or her. Even if the workplace really needed to get in touch with someone, doing so might have been impossible. Cell phones did not exist. When people were driving, shopping, outdoors, or traveling, it was very difficult to reach them. The message had to wait until the person returned home.

Digital communications and smartphones changed everything. Sherry Turkle says, "Connectivity technologies once promised to give us more time. But as the cell phone and smartphone eroded the boundaries between work and leisure, all the time in the world was not enough."[58] The fact that people can connect to each other more quickly and easily does save time on each communication. But it also multiplies the number of communications possible, effectively chopping up time into tinier and tinier pieces.

> "We are no longer constrained by the walls of an office. We can work anytime anywhere."[59]
>
> —Robert Grove, CEO of Edelman Hong Kong

Space has changed as well. No matter where people go today, they have the power to show up virtually at almost any other place. This has enormous benefits for families, friends, and businesses separated by long distances. Regular connection can help enhance relationships and improve productivity. "The workplace has become somewhat borderless," says Robert Grove, CEO of Edelman Hong Kong, a marketing firm. "We are no longer constrained by the walls of an office. We can work anytime anywhere."[59]

People who can work anytime and anywhere often do exactly that, blurring the distinction between being at home, on vacation, or at work. This may feel freeing or stressful, depending on the situation. In 2016 a Lyft driver named Mary decided to pick up riders in Chicago while nine months pregnant. Her due date was a week away, but she started to feel some labor pains. According to a Lyft blog post, "Since she didn't believe she was going into labor yet, she stayed in driver mode, and sure enough—ping!— she received a ride request en route to the hospital."[60] After drop-

Before the digital revolution, when a person left work, it was not easy or polite for a boss or coworker to contact them. Today people are always available, blurring the lines between work and personal time.

ping off that passenger, Mary went to the hospital and gave birth to a baby girl. Lyft presented the story as exciting and inspiring. But many who read it disagreed. They saw this as proof that we live in a society that celebrates overwork. Most people agree that someone should not feel compelled to work while going through something like childbirth.

Fear of Missing Out

Yet people do feel compelled to work and otherwise engage with the digital world almost all of the time. News from friends, family, the local area, and the rest of the world is available around the

When Private Files Go Public

In the past getting at someone's private photos meant breaking into their home or office. Today private digital files get hacked or leaked all the time. But that does not make the invasion any less devastating. In 2014 hackers targeted several celebrities' private Apple iCloud accounts. They managed to get into Jennifer Lawrence's private account and found nude pictures of the actress, who starred in *The Hunger Games* and *X Men*. "It was so unbelievably violating that you can't even put [it] into words," she said in 2017, adding that she is still recovering from the incident. She continued, "There was not one person in the world that is not capable of seeing these intimate photos of me."

Apple looked into the incident and said that the attackers may have gained access through figuring out easy-to-guess passwords or by sending official-looking messages asking for user names or passwords. This is called phishing. No matter how the hackers got in, the theft was a crime. Sharing someone's private information online without permission is never acceptable.

Quoted in Maya Oppenheim, "Jennifer Lawrence Addresses Nude Photo Hack: 'It Was So Unbelievably Violating,'" *Independent* (London), November 21, 2017. www.independent.co.uk.

clock. And keeping up one's social standing means contributing to that stream of news quickly and regularly. Every person who participates in social media has become a news reporter, radio station, and TV channel all rolled into one. For many people a smartphone or tablet is the last thing they look at before going to bed and the first thing they look at when waking up. A 2013 study by the research firm IDC found that 79 percent of smartphone users in the United States check their device within fifteen minutes of waking up, and 62 percent check it immediately. This obsessive checking typically continues throughout the day, while shopping, working out, cooking, or working.

Young people have a word for what drives this behavior: *FoMO*, short for "fear of missing out." People experience FoMO when they feel anxious or overwhelmed about what others might know that they do not or about what others might be doing without their involvement. Nobody likes to feel left out, but in a world awash with constant news and information, it is impossible to pay attention to everything. Trying too hard to keep up with the digital world may cause the real world and the real self to pale in comparison. "When you're so tuned in to the 'other,' or the 'better' (in your mind), you lose your authentic sense of self,"[61] says Darlene McLaughlin, a psychiatrist at the Texas A&M Health Science Center College of Medicine.

Digital technology is changing people's identities as well as their sense of time and space. It is tearing down the walls between private and public and between home and work. But disengaging from digital technology to avoid an invasion of privacy is not an option. Digital technology is fun, exciting, and necessary for participating in society today. People must find ways to integrate the digital world into their lives without losing themselves in the process.

CHAPTER FIVE

Welcome to the Future

A teen boy wakes up and a voice speaks in his ear through a digital implant. The voice alerts him to any important or interesting messages that arrived while he was asleep and tells him the weather forecast. The boy showers, and as he bathes, a camera in the shower head works together with tiny sensors embedded in his body to assess his health and wellness. Meanwhile, the kitchen knows he is awake. A robotic system is already preparing his breakfast, which contains items specifically chosen for his nutritional needs, as assessed by the health system. When the boy is ready for the day, he walks into an empty room. But it does not stay empty for long. His digital implant projects a new reality. The space around him seems to transform into the surface of Mars. The boy is studying outer space. He learns at his own pace through virtual experiences specially targeted toward his interests and level of understanding.

Altered Reality

This boy's experience is completely fictional. However, advances in digital technology could make a scenario like this possible. One important feature of this story is that digital technology has become completely integrated into the boy's life and body—he is never offline. His constant digital connection has become like a sixth sense, an ability akin to sight or hearing that he relies on in order to understand and react to his world. From his point of view, it would not really make sense to distinguish between the digital constructs and the physical world. Both are equally real to him.

The real world and the Internet are already beginning to merge. Virtual reality technology makes an online experience seem much more real with 360-degree vision and sound, touch sensations, and more. Meanwhile, augmented reality overlays digital media onto the real world through holograms or projections. "We will grow accustomed to seeing the world through multiple data layers,"[62] predicts Daren C. Brabham, a professor at the Annenberg School for Communication and Journalism. Screens could one day disappear from people's lives. It may become much more normal to interact with technology through speech and gestures.

Virtual and augmented reality give people instant access to experiences. Police, soldiers, and emergency personnel are already using these technologies to train in extremely realistic scenarios. It may soon become commonplace to watch a concert or football game from a virtual front-row seat. Eventually, a grandmother who falls sick and cannot attend her grandson's birthday celebration could relive the recorded party once she recovers. Virtual or augmented interactions could help restore some of the depth and authenticity missing from today's digital interactions.

Experts believe that technology will continue to radically change people's lives. Rather than read about Mars, for example, a student may be projected into a virtual exploration of its surface.

A conversation in virtual reality or with a hologram projection of a friend would likely feel more like being with the person in real life.

The Internet of Things

As virtual and augmented reality technologies bring online experiences into the real world, the Internet of Things (IoT) is bringing more and more of the physical world online. The original Internet was like a virtual library, storing information for easy access. The IoT is more like a brain. It collects, combines, and analyzes information. The IoT grows as more objects gain connectivity. Most modern cars come with GPS systems and can pair with the driver's smartphone to provide access to apps. Fitbits and smart watches monitor people's health and fitness. Home assistants such as Amazon's Alexa take voice commands to play music or make purchases.

In addition, a variety of sensors, cameras, and other monitoring devices continuously collect data from many parts of the real

Big Brother Is Watching

Many people use the phrase "Big Brother is watching" to describe a level of surveillance that feels creepy or invasive. The line comes from a classic science fiction novel, *Nineteen Eighty-Four* by George Orwell, originally published in 1949. Orwell imagined a future in which an organization called the Party, led by a mysterious figure called Big Brother, oversees and controls everything the citizens do. The Party uses technology and a fleet of undercover officers called the Thought Police to watch every citizen all the time. It is illegal to act or even think in a manner counter to the interests of the Party, which fabricates its own version of reality and its own language, called Newspeak. People are taught not to trust their own eyes and ears. Instead, as Orwell writes, "Whatever the Party holds to be truth is truth." The main character's job is rewriting old documents, changing these records of what happened to fit the Party's interests.

Quoted in Michiko Kakutani, "Why '1984' Is a 2017 Must-Read," *New York Times*, January 26, 2017. www.nytimes.com.

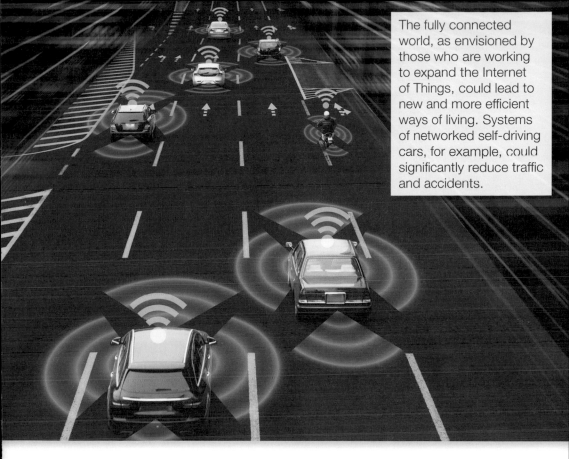

The fully connected world, as envisioned by those who are working to expand the Internet of Things, could lead to new and more efficient ways of living. Systems of networked self-driving cars, for example, could significantly reduce traffic and accidents.

world and share that information with computer systems in real time. This is leading to the digitization of entire industries. When all the parts of a system communicate effectively to make decisions as a group, the system runs more smoothly. For example, sensors already keep tabs on crops in some farmers' fields, allowing for a system that automatically waters or fertilizes a field only when necessary. Some cities have experimented with Internet-connected sensors in parking lots to help direct people to open spaces.

In the future, the possibilities are endless. "Anything that can be connected, will be connected,"[63] predicts Jacob Morgan, author of *The Future of Work: Attract New Talent, Build Better Leaders, and Create a Competitive Organization*. Systems of networked self-driving cars could communicate with each other

> "Anything that can be connected, will be connected."[63]
>
> —Jacob Morgan, author of *The Future of Work: Attract New Talent, Build Better Leaders, and Create a Competitive Organization*

and share information to figure out the most efficient routes for each car, saving time and energy. The United States is working on overhauling its electrical grid with sensors and other technology to help make the system more aware of how energy is being used. Then power can be distributed more efficiently. Buildings and even entire cities could use smart systems to help improve energy efficiency, water usage, waste management, and more.

Predicting the Future

Some smart systems use AI to make decisions automatically. David Clark, a research scientist at MIT, says, "More and more, humans will be in a world in which decisions are being made by an active set of cooperating devices."[64] These systems can anticipate people's needs. Algorithms already suggest new friends on Facebook; come up with books, movies, music, and other products people might enjoy; and even diagnose cancer and suggest treatment plans. Eventually, algorithms with access to enough data about a person's body could predict a medical condition before it occurs. Similarly, data on social interactions and behavior could someday feed into an algorithm that predicts future crimes or conflicts.

> "More and more, humans will be in a world in which decisions are being made by an active set of cooperating devices."[64]
>
> —David Clark, research scientist, MIT

Connecting the world together via the IoT into smart systems improves productivity and efficiency but compromises privacy and safety. "The IoT reality represents both huge opportunity and huge vulnerability. They go hand in hand,"[65] says Barry Chudakov, founder of Sertain Research, a marketing technology company. The IoT is vulnerable to a targeted attack or to a natural disaster that damages its ability to gather data or communicate that data. In addition, governments or organizations with the power to tap into a smart system's data could use that information for surveillance or population control. "In the future, intelligence services might use the [IoT] for identification, surveillance,

A Smart City

Singapore, a small nation consisting of a single city on an island in Southeast Asia, has turned itself into one of the world's first smart cities. Its Smart Nation initiative is actively testing out a variety of digital solutions meant to improve housing, health, and transportation. "In Singapore, we know that new technology trumps politics as usual," says Dr. Vivian Balakrishnan, the country's minister for foreign affairs, who also leads the Smart Nation initiative.

In one neighborhood in the city, thousands of sensors on people's apartments measure how much water and energy they use and how much waste they throw away. This feedback helps people save resources and helps the government design more effective programs. On the streets of Singapore, self-driving taxis and buses already shuttle people around. The city imposes high taxes on private cars, so most people rely on public transportation. By 2020 the city plans to require all vehicles in the city to use the same navigation system. The system will keep track of where every car in the city is at all times. Authorities will be able to monitor traffic conditions and watch for problems in real time.

Quoted in Aaron Souppouris, "Singapore Is Striving to Be the World's First 'Smart City,'" *Engadget* (blog), November 3, 2016. www.engadget.com.

monitoring, location tracking, and targeting for recruitment, or to gain access to networks or user credentials,"[66] says James Clapper, former director of national intelligence. Maybe the boy in the fictional story at the beginning of this chapter knows that his government is watching his every move and will step in immediately if he misbehaves.

A Society Divided

As digital technology advances, people with access to digital devices and companies that engineer smart systems will become ever more wealthy and powerful, while those without access will become poorer and more dependent on others. This "digital divide" already exists. Wealthier, more educated people

> "The IoT reality represents both huge opportunity and huge vulnerability. They go hand in hand."[65]
>
> —Barry Chudakov, founder of Sertain Research

have the means to purchase digital devices and develop technical skills. Meanwhile, impoverished people or those living in rural areas or developing countries may not have access to the best, most useful technology. Experts predict that this divide will only worsen with time as those with power develop smart systems to benefit themselves. "Networked transactions . . . benefit smaller and smaller segments of the global population,"[67] says Oscar Gandy, who studies information and public policy at the Annenberg School for Communication at the University of Pennsylvania.

At the same time, the global population will become ever more aware of this divide. As more people gain Internet access and communicate with each other on social media, they will realize what is going on. They will see how smart systems are benefiting the wealthy and the powerful but not the weak or disadvantaged. "The anger, hostility, and resentment that will be generated in response to this inequality seem likely to be expressed in ways that will cause great and lasting harm,"[68] says Gandy. Disadvantaged and disgruntled people could use social media to connect and organize protests and revolutions that shake the foundations of society. This conflict could resolve in several ways. On the negative side, an oppressive, controlling regime could use surveillance tools to weed out dissenters and squash rebellions. "We are creating a society by which a totalitarian government can control everything. Right now it's more power to the powerful,"[69] says Bruce Schneier, a security expert and chief technology officer at IBM Resilient.

A World United

But it is also possible that hierarchical leadership could collapse. As people all around the world connect and share ideas, they may be able to act quickly to organize solutions to problems from the ground up. Most companies and governments today instead take a top-down approach to change. JP Rangaswami, chief scientist at Salesforce.com, says that this approach tends to get bogged down in conferences and committees. He says that current systems of government are not well equipped to establish smart systems or act on insights gained from these systems. Instead, real problem solving may come from regular people who rise up and work together. "We have many opportunities to solve significant problems of education, health care, democracy, and promoting freedom throughout the world,"[70] says Glenn Edens, a research scientist at Palo Alto Research Center, a technical consulting firm.

Digital technology has the power to greatly amplify both the good and the bad in humanity. From virtual and augmented reality to big data and the IoT, emerging digital tools will make it ever easier for people to connect and support each other or to exclude and control each other. To make the most of these new tools, people need to take digital technology seriously. In the midst of each frenzied day, they must preserve time and space for caring for their relationships with each other. At the same time, they must adapt nimbly to ever-changing ways of doing business and running society. They must also think clearly and critically about the information they consume. And finally, they must take responsibility for their own futures.

SOURCE NOTES

Introduction: A Whole New World

1. Quoted in Katrina Schwartz, "What Happens When Teens Try to Disconnect from Tech for Three Days," KQED, March 6, 2015. https://ww2.kqed.org.
2. Quoted in Rosie Ifould, "'I Worried People Would Forget About Me': Can Teenagers Survive Without Social Media?," *Guardian* (Manchester), June 18, 2016. www.theguardian.com.
3. Quoted in Lee Rainie and Janna Anderson, "The Internet of Things Connectivity Binge: What Are the Implications?," Pew Research Center, June 6, 2017. www.pewinternet.org.

Chapter One: Real Relationships

4. Quoted in Ifould, "'I Worried People Would Forget About Me.'"
5. Sherry Turkle, *Alone Together: Why We Expect More from Technology and Less from Each Other*. New York: Basic Books, 2012, Kindle edition, p. 12.
6. Quoted in Maura Keller, "Social Media and Interpersonal Communication," *Social Work Today*, May/June 2013, p. 10. www.socialworktoday.com.
7. Turkle, *Alone Together*, p. 1.
8. Quoted in Eric M. Strauss et al., "How This Teen Fell into a World of Secret Sexting, Alcohol and Drugs," ABC News, May 16, 2017. http://abcnews.go.com.
9. Quoted in Molly Soat, "Social Media Triggers a Dopamine High," American Marketing Association, November 2015. www.ama.org.
10. Turkle, *Alone Together*, p. 13.
11. Quoted in Sarah Marsh, "Girls and Social Media: 'You Are Expected to Live Up to an Impossible Standard,'" *Guardian* (Manchester), August 22, 2017. www.theguardian.com.
12. Quoted in Marsh, "Girls and Social Media."
13. Quoted in Marsh, "Girls and Social Media."
14. Alex Lickerman, "The Effect of Technology on Relationships," *Happiness in This World* (blog), *Psychology Today*, June 8, 2010. www.psychologytoday.com.

15. Quoted in Michigan News, "Empathy: College Students Don't Have as Much as They Used To," May 27, 2010. http://ns.umich.edu.
16. Lickerman, "The Effect of Technology on Relationships."
17. Quoted in Cyberbullying Research Center, "What Is Cyberbullying?" https://cyberbullying.org.
18. Quoted in Keller, "Social Media and Interpersonal Communication."
19. Quoted in Amanda MacMillan, "The Surprising Power of Facebook Comments—According to Science," *Real Simple*, 2018. www.realsimple.com.
20. Quoted in Monica Garske, "UC San Diego Study Shows Facebook Feelings Are Contagious," 7 San Diego, March 12, 2014. www.nbcsandiego.com.
21. Quoted in Kathryn Hulick, "Twitch Together," *Muse*, April 2017, p. 39.
22. Quoted in Paul Kerley, "The Graphs That Show the Search for Love Has Changed," BBC, February 13, 2016. www.bbc.com.

Chapter Two: A Sharing Society

23. Quoted in Uptin Saiidi, "Millennials Are Prioritizing 'Experiences' over Stuff," CNBC, May 5, 2016. www.cnbc.com.
24. Jeremy Rifkin, *The Zero Marginal Cost Society: The Internet of Things, the Collaborative Commons, and the Eclipse of Capitalism*. St. Martin's Griffin, 2015, p. 233.
25. Quoted in Jason Tanz, "How Airbnb and Lyft Finally Got Americans to Trust Each Other," *Wired*, April 23, 2014. www.wired.com.
26. Quoted in Tanz, "How Airbnb and Lyft Finally Got Americans to Trust Each Other."
27. Quoted in Tanz, "How Airbnb and Lyft Finally Got Americans to Trust Each Other."
28. Tomas Chamorro-Premuzic, "Reputation and the Rise of the 'Rating' Society," *Guardian* (Manchester), October 26, 2015. www.theguardian.com.
29. Quoted in Josh Dzieza, "The Rating Game," Verge, October 28, 2015. www.verge.com.
30. Quoted in Shankar Vedantam, "New Research Looks at Ways to Help Stop Airbnb Racial Discrimination," NPR, March 2, 2017. www.npr.org.

31. Quoted in Tamar Lewin, "Instruction for Masses Knocks Down Campus Walls," *New York Times*, March 4, 2012. www.nytimes.com.
32. Quoted in Chris Lefkow, "Social Media, Cellphone Video Fuel Arab Protests," *Sydney Morning Herald*, February 22, 2011. www.smh.com.au.

Chapter Three: Information Overload

33. Quoted in Nicholas Carr, *The Shallows: What the Internet Is Doing to Our Brains*. New York: Norton, 2011, p. 6.
34. Quoted in Mara Hvistendahl, "Inside China's Vast New Experiment in Social Ranking," *Wired*, December 14, 2017. www.wired.com.
35. Quoted in Glenn Greenwald et al., "Edward Snowden: The Whistleblower Behind the NSA Surveillance Revelations," *Guardian* (Manchester), June 11, 2013. www.theguardian.com.
36. Quoted in Veronica Ma, "Propaganda and Censorship: Adapting to the Modern Age," *Harvard International Review*, April 28, 2016. http://hir.harvard.edu.
37. Quoted in Jackie Wattles, "Net Neutrality Repeal: Facebook, Amazon, Netflix and Internet Providers React," CNNMoney, December 14, 2017. http://money.cnn.com.
38. Quoted in Mike Wendling, "The (Almost) Complete History of 'Fake News,'" *Trending* (blog), BBC, January 22, 2018. www.bbc.com.
39. Quoted in Charlie Warzel, "He Predicted the 2016 Fake News Crisis. Now He's Worried About an Information Apocalypse," BuzzFeed, February 11, 2018. www.buzzfeed.com.
40. Quoted in Maggie Haberman and Jonathan Martin, "Trump Once Said the 'Access Hollywood' Tape Was Real. Now He's Not Sure," *New York Times*, November 28, 2017. www.nytimes.com.
41. Quoted in Warzel, "He Predicted the 2016 Fake News Crisis."
42. Quoted in Tom Nichols, "America's Cult of Ignorance," *Daily Beast*, April 1, 2017. www.thedailybeast.com.
43. Quoted in Janna Anderson and Lee Rainie, "The Future of Truth and Misinformation Online," Pew Research Center, October 19, 2017. www.pewinternet.org.
44. Quoted in Anderson and Rainie, "The Future of Truth and Misinformation Online."

45. Quoted in Tim Elmore, "Why Empathy Is Declining Among Students and What We Can Do," *Artificial Maturity* (blog), *Psychology Today*, March 20, 2014. www.psychologytoday .com.

46. Nicholas Carr, *The Shallows: What the Internet Is Doing to Our Brains*. New York: Norton, 2011, p. 7.

47. Quoted in Tanya Lewis, "Here's What Science Says About How Digital Technology REALLY Affects Our Brains," Business Insider, August 12, 2015. www.businessinsider.com.

48. George Lakoff, *Don't Think of an Elephant*. White River Junction, VT: Chelsea Green, 2004, p. 17.

Chapter Four: Identity Dilemma

49. Quoted in Elizabeth Day, "How Selfies Became a Global Phenomenon," *Guardian* (Manchester), July 13, 2013. www.the guardian.com.

50. Quoted in Day, "How Selfies Became a Global Phenomenon."

51. Quoted in Day, "How Selfies Became a Global Phenomenon."

52. Quoted in Cox News Service, "Middle-School Kids Using Social Media to Experiment with Identity," *Denver (CO) Post*, August 26, 2011. www.denverpost.com.

53. John Palfrey and Urs Gasser, *Born Digital: How Children Grow Up in a Digital Age*. New York: Basic Books, 2016, p. 52.

54. Quoted in Kashmir Hill, "Facebook Recommended That This Psychiatrist's Patients Friend Each Other," *Splinter*, August 29, 2016. https://splinternews.com.

55. Quoted in Hill, "Facebook Recommended That This Psychiatrist's Patients Friend Each Other."

56. Quoted in Nick Statt, "Mark Zuckerberg Apologizes for Facebook's Data Privacy Scandal in Full-Page Newspaper Ads," Verge, March 25, 2018. www.theverge.com.

57. Andrew Burt and Dan Geer, "The End of Privacy," *New York Times*, October 5, 2017. www.nytimes.com.

58. Turkle, *Alone Together*, p. 13.

59. Quoted in Claudio Cocorocchia, "How the Digitization of Work Affects Us All," World Economic Forum, January 19, 2016. www.weforum.org.

60. Quoted in Jia Tolentino, "The Gig Economy Celebrates Working Yourself to Death," *New Yorker*, March 22, 2017. www .newyorker.com.

61. Quoted in Texas A&M University, "FOMO: It's Your Life You're Missing Out On," ScienceDaily, March 30, 2016. www.sci encedaily.com.

Chapter Five: Welcome to the Future

62. Quoted in Janna Anderson and Lee Rainie, "Summary: 15 Theses About the Digital Future," Pew Research Center, March 11, 2014. www.pewinternet.org.
63. Jacob Morgan, "A Simple Explanation of 'the Internet of Things,'" *Forbes*, May 13, 2014. www.forbes.com.
64. Quoted in Anderson and Rainie, "Summary."
65. Quoted in Rainie and Anderson, "The Internet of Things Connectivity Binge."
66. Quoted in Spencer Ackerman and Sam Thielman, "US Intelligence Chief: We Might Use the Internet of Things to Spy on You," *Guardian* (Manchester), February 9, 2016. www.the guardian.com.
67. Quoted in Anderson and Rainie, "Summary."
68. Quoted in Anderson and Rainie, "Summary."
69. Quoted in Rainie and Anderson, "The Internet of Things Connectivity Binge."
70. Quoted in Janna Anderson and Lee Rainie, "The Less-Hopeful Theses," Pew Research Center, March 11, 2014. www.pew internet.org.

ORGANIZATIONS TO CONTACT

Center for Digital Democracy
1621 Connecticut Ave., Suite 550
Washington, DC 20009
website: www.democraticmedia.org

The Center for Digital Democracy is a leading consumer protection and privacy organization that was founded in 2001. Its website offers press releases, information about its current projects, a special section on youth privacy and digital marketing, and link to the *Need to Know* blog.

Federal Communications Commission (FCC)
445 Twelfth St. SW
Washington, DC 20554
website: www.fcc.gov

The FCC is an independent US government agency that regulates communications by radio, television, wire, satellite, and cable in all fifty states, the District of Columbia, and US territories. Numerous publications related to online privacy issues can be accessed through the website's search engine.

Internet Society
1775 Wiehle Ave.
Reston, VA 20190
website: www.internetsociety.org

The Internet Society is an organization devoted to increasing Internet access around the world and ensuring that the Internet remains free, transparent, and open to all.

National Cyber Security Alliance
1010 Vermont Ave. NW
Washington, DC 20005
website: http://staysafeonline.org

Through education and awareness efforts, the National Cyber Security Alliance seeks to inform and empower individuals to use the Internet safely and securely. Numerous publications related to online privacy can be accessed through the website's search engine.

World Economic Forum
91-93 route de la Capite
CH-1223 Cologny/Geneva
Switzerland
website: www.weforum.org

The World Economic Forum works to improve the state of the world through cooperation between governments, organizations, and private groups. The group asserts that all organizations must be accountable to all parts of society.

World Privacy Forum
3108 Fifth Ave., Suite B
San Diego, CA 92103
website: www.worldprivacyforum.org

Through independent privacy research, analysis, and consumer education, the World Privacy Forum seeks to empower people with the knowledge and tools they need to protect their online privacy. Its website offers reports, congressional testimonies, news releases, health privacy publications, and an alphabetized Key Issues section.

FOR FURTHER RESEARCH

Books

Nancy Baym, *Personal Connections in the Digital Age*. Malden, MA: Polity, 2016.

Susan Greenfield, *Mind Change: How Digital Technologies Are Leaving Their Mark on Our Brains*. New York: Random House, 2015.

Carla Mooney, *How the Internet Is Changing Society*. San Diego, CA: ReferencePoint, 2016.

John Palfrey and Urs Gasser, *Born Digital: How Children Grow Up in a Digital Age*. New York: Basic Books, 2016.

Jeremy Rifkin, *The Zero Marginal Cost Society: The Internet of Things, the Collaborative Commons, and the Eclipse of Capitalism*. New York: St. Martin's Griffin, 2015.

Sherry Turkle, *Reclaiming Conversation: The Power of Talk in a Digital Age*. New York: Penguin, 2015.

Internet Sources

Janna Anderson and Lee Rainie, "The Future of Truth and Misinformation Online," Pew Research Center, October 19, 2017. www.pewinternet.org/2017/10/19/the-future-of-truth-and-misinformation-online.

Josh Dzieza, "The Rating Game," Verge, October 28, 2015. www.theverge.com/2015/10/28/9625968/rating-system-on-demand-economy-uber-olive-garden.

Rosie Ifould, "'I Worried People Would Forget About Me': Can Teenagers Survive Without Social Media?," *Guardian* (Manchester), June 18, 2016. www.theguardian.com/media/2016/jun/18/can-teenagers-survive-without-social-media.

Veronica Ma, "Propaganda and Censorship: Adapting to the Modern Age," *Harvard International Review*, April 28, 2016. http://hir.harvard.edu/article/?a=13083.

Sarah Marsh, "Girls and Social Media: 'You Are Expected to Live Up to an Impossible Standard,'" *Guardian* (Manchester), August 22, 2017. www.theguardian.com/society/2017/aug/23/girls-and -social-media-you-are-expected-to-live-up-to-an-impossible -standard.

Lee Rainie and Janna Anderson, "The Internet of Things Connectivity Binge: What Are the Implications?," Pew Research Center, June 6, 2017. www.pewinternet.org/2017/06/06/the-internet-of -things-connectivity-binge-what-are-the-implications.

Uptin Saiidi, "Millennials Are Prioritizing 'Experiences' over Stuff," CNBC, May 5, 2016. www.cnbc.com/2016/05/05/millennials -are-prioritizing-experiences-over-stuff.html.

Charlie Warzel, "He Predicted the 2016 Fake News Crisis. Now He's Worried About an Information Apocalypse," BuzzFeed, February 11, 2018. www.buzzfeed.com/charliewarzel/the-terrifying -future-of-fake-news?utm_term=.fcQve5NJJ#.updmrv833.

Websites

Addiction.com (www.addiction.com). This website provides information on various addictions, including the compulsive use of the Internet, technology, or video games. Resources are provided for people who are seeking help for themselves or a loved one.

FactCheck.org (www.factcheck.org). From the Annenberg Public Policy Center of the University of Pennsylvania, this nonprofit site aims to reduce confusion surrounding political messages by providing nonbiased, factual analysis of political ads, debates, speeches, interviews, and press releases.

NetSmartz (www.netsmartz.org). From the National Center for Missing and Exploited Children, this site has information about topics that relate to privacy and social media, including cyberbullying, social networking, and more.

Pew Research Center: Internet & Technology (www.pew internet.org). The Pew Research Center conducts surveys, data analysis, and social science research to inform the public about key issues. The Internet and technology is one of its key areas of focus.

Snopes (www.snopes.com). This site provides fact-checking and background information for any legends or rumors circulating online in an attempt to separate facts from falsehoods.

StaySafeOnline (https://staysafeonline.org). From the National Cyber Security Alliance, this site offers information and tools to help people use the Internet safely and securely at home, work, and school.

StopBullying.gov (www.stopbullying.gov). From the US Department of Health and Human Services, this website is devoted to helping children, teens, and their parents handle cases of cyberbullying.

INDEX

PICTURE CREDITS